ON THE PSYCHICAL MECHANISM OF HYSTERICAL PHENOMENA

BY

SIGMUND FREUD

British Library Cataloguing-in-Publication Data
A catalogue record for this book is available from the
British Library

Contents

Sigmund Freud

Sigismund Schlomo Freud was born on 6th May 1856, in the Moravian town of Příbor, now part of the Czech Republic.

Sigmund was the eldest of eight children to Jewish Galician parents, Jacob and Amalia Freud. After Freud's father lost his business as a result of the Panic of 1857, the family were forced to move to Leipzig and then Vienna to avoid poverty. It was in Vienna that the nine-year-old Sigmund enrolled at the Leopoldstädter Kommunal-Realgymnasium before beginning his medical training at the University of Vienna in 1873, at the age of just 17. He studied a variety of subjects, including philosophy, physiology, and zoology, graduating with an MD in 1881.

The following year, Freud began his medical career in Theodor Meynert's psychiatric clinic at the Vienna General Hospital. He worked there until 1886 when he set up in private practice and began specialising in "nervous disorders". In the same year he married Merth Bernays, with whom he had 6 children between 1887 and 1895.

In the period between 1896 and 1901, Freud isolated himself from his colleagues and began work on developing the basics of his psychoanalytic theory. He published *The Interpretation of Dreams*, in 1899, to a lacklustre reception, but continued to produce works such as *The Psychopathology of Everyday Life* (1901) and *Three Essays on the Theory of Sexuality* (1905). He held a weekly meeting at his home known as the "Wednesday Psychological Society" which eventually developed into the Vienna Psycho-Analytic Society. His ideas gained momentum and by the end of the decade his methods were being used internationally by neurologists and psychiatrists.

Freud made a huge and lasting contribution to the field of psychology with many of his methods still being used in modern psychoanalysis. He inspired much discussion on the wealth of theories he produced and the reactions to his works began a century of great psychological investigation.

In 1930 Freud fled Vienna due to rise of Nazism and resided in England until his death from mouth cancer on 23rd September 1939.

ON THE PSYCHICAL MECHANISM OF HYSTERICAL PHENOMENA (1893)

Gentlemen, - I am appearing before you to-day with the object of giving you a report on a work the first part of which has already been published in the *Zentralblatt für Neurologie* under the names of Josef Breuer and myself. As you may gather from the title of the work, it deals with the pathogenesis of hysterical symptoms and suggests that the immediate reasons for the development of hysterical symptoms are to be looked for in the sphere of psychical life.

But before I enter further into the contents of this joint work, I must explain the position it occupies and name the author and the discovery which, in substance at least, we have taken as our starting point, although our contribution has been developed quite independently.

As you know, Gentlemen, all the modern advances made in the understanding and knowledge of hysteria are derived from the work of Charcot. In the first half of the eighties, Charcot began to turn his attention to the 'major neurosis', as the French call hysteria. In a series of researches he has succeeded in proving the presence of regularity and law where the inadequate or half-hearted clinical observations of other people saw only malingering or a puzzling lack of conformity to rule. It may safely be said that everything new that has been learnt about hysteria in recent times goes back directly or indirectly to his suggestions. But among Charcot's numerous works, none, in my estimate, is of higher value than the one in which he taught us to understand the traumatic paralyses which appear in hysteria; and since it is precisely this work of which ours appears as a continuation, I hope you will allow me to lay this subject before you once again in some detail.

[1] A lecture delivered by Dr. Sigm. Freud at a meeting of the 'Wiener medizinischer Club' on January 11, 1893. Special shorthand report by the *Wiener medizinische Presse*, revised by the lecturer.

We will take the case of a person who is subjected to a trauma without having been ill previously and perhaps without ever having any hereditary taint. The trauma must fulfil certain conditions. It must be severe - that is, it must be of a kind involving the idea of mortal danger, of a threat to life. But it must not be severe in the sense of bringing psychical activity to an end. Otherwise it will not produce the result we expect from it. Thus, for instance, it must not involve concussion of the brain or any really serious injury. Moreover, the trauma must have a special relation to some part of the body. Let us suppose that a heavy billet of wood falls on a workman's shoulder The blow knocks him down, but he soon realizes that nothing has happened and goes home with a slight contusion. After a few weeks, or after some months, he wakes up one morning and notices that the arm that was subjected to the trauma is hanging down limp and paralysed, though in the interval, in what might be called the incubation period, he has made perfectly good use of it. If the case is a typical one, it may happen that peculiar attacks set in - that, after an aura, the subject suddenly collapses, raves, and becomes delirious; and, if he speaks in his delirium, what he says may show that the scene of his accident is being repeated in him, embellished, perhaps, with various imaginary pictures. What has been happening here? How is this phenomenon to be explained?

Charcot explains the process by reproducing it, by inducing the paralysis in a patient artificially. In order to bring this about, he needs a patient who is already in a hysterical state; he further requires the condition of hypnosis and the method of suggestion. He puts a patient of this kind into deep hypnosis and gives him a light blow on the arm. The arm drops; it is paralysed and shows precisely the same symptoms as occur in spontaneous traumatic paralysis. The blow may also be replaced by a direct verbal suggestion: 'Look! your arm is paralysed!' In this case too the paralysis exhibits the same characteristics.

Let us try to compare the two cases :on the one hand a trauma, on the other a traumatic suggestion. The final result, the paralysis, is exactly the same in both cases. If the trauma in the one case can be replaced in the other case by a verbal suggestion, it is plausible to suppose that an idea of this kind was responsible for the development of the paralysis in the case of the spontaneous traumatic paralysis as well. And in fact a number of patients report that at the moment of the trauma they actually had a feeling that their arm was smashed. If this were so, the trauma could really be completely equated with the verbal suggestion. But to complete the analogy a third factor is required. In order that the idea 'your arm is paralysed' should be able to provoke a paralysis in the patient, it was necessary for him to be in a state of hypnosis. But the workman was not in a state of hypnosis. Nevertheless, we may assume that he was in a special state of mind during the trauma; and Charcot is inclined to equate that affect with the artificially induced state of hypnosis. This being so, the traumatic spontaneous paralysis is completely explained and brought into line with the paralysis produced by suggestion; and the genesis of the symptom is unambiguously determined by the circumstances of the trauma.

Charcot has, moreover, repeated the same experiment in order to explain the contractures and pains which appear in traumatic hysteria; and in my opinion there is scarcely any point at which he has penetrated into the understanding of hysteria more deeply than here. But his analysis goes no further: we do not learn how other symptoms are generated, and above all we do not learn how hysterical symptoms come about in common, non-traumatic hysteria.

At about the same time, Gentlemen, at which Charcot was thus throwing light on hystero-traumatic paralyses, Dr. Breuer between 1880 and 1882, undertook the medical care of a young lady who - with a non-traumatic aetiology - fell ill of a severe and complicated hysteria (accompanied by paralyses, contractures, disturbances of speech and vision, and psychical peculiarities of every kind), while she was nursing her sick father. This case will retain an important place in the history of hysteria, since it was the first one in which a physician succeeded in elucidating all the symptoms of the hysterical state, in learning the origin of each symptom and at the same time in finding a means of causing that symptom to disappear We may say that it was the first case of hysteria to be made intelligible. Dr. Breuer kept back the conclusions which followed from this case till he could be certain that it did not stand alone. After I returned, in 1886, from a course of study under Charcot, I began, with Breuer's constant co-operation, to make close observations on a fairly large number of hysterical patients and to examine them from this point of view; and I found that the behaviour of this first patient had in fact been typical and that the inferences which were justified by that case could be carried over to a considerable number of hysterical patients, if not to all.

Our material consisted of cases of common, that is of non-traumatic, hysteria. Our procedure was to take each separate symptom and enquire into the circumstances in which it had made its first appearance; and we endeavoured in this way to arrive at a clear idea of the precipitating cause that symptom. Now you must not suppose that this is a simple job. If you question patients along these lines, you will as a rule receive no answer at all to begin with. In a small group of cases the patients have their reasons for not saying what they know. But in a greater number of cases the patients have no notion of the context of their symptoms. The method by which something can be learnt is an arduous one. It is as follows. The patients must be put under hypnosis and then questioned as to the origin of some particular symptom - as to when it first appeared and what they remember in that connection. While they are in this state, the memory, which was not at their disposal in a waking state, returns. We have learnt in this manner that, to put it roughly, there is an affectively coloured experience behind most, if not all, phenomena of hysteria; and further, that this experience is of such a kind that it at once makes the symptom to which it relates intelligible and shows accordingly that the symptom, once again, is unambiguously determined. If you will allow me to equate this affectively coloured experience with the major traumatic experience underlying traumatic hysteria, I can at once formulate the first thesis at which we have arrived: '*There is a complete analogy between traumatic paralysis and common, non-traumatic hysteria.*' The only difference is that in the former a major trauma has been operative, whereas in the latter there is seldom a *single* major event to be signalized, but rather a *series* of affective impressions - a whole story of suffering. But there is nothing forced in equating such a story, which appears as the determining factor in hysterical patients, with the accident which occurs in traumatic hysteria. For no one doubts any longer to-day that even in the case of the major mechanical trauma in traumatic hysteria what produces the result is not the mechanical factor but the affect of fright, the *psychical* trauma. The first thing that follows from all this, then, is that the pattern of traumatic hysteria, as it was laid down by Charcot for hysterical paralyses, applies quite generally to all hysterical phenomena, or at least to the great majority of them. In every case what we have to deal with is the operation of psychical traumas, which unambiguously determine the nature of the symptoms that arise.

I will now give you a few instances of this. First, here is an example of the occurrence of contractures. Throughout the whole period of her illness, Breuer's patient, whom I have already mentioned, exhibited a contracture of the right arm. It emerged under hypnosis that at a time before she had fallen ill she was subjected to the following trauma. She was sitting half-dozing at the bedside of her sick father; her right arm was hanging over the back of her chair and went to sleep. At this moment she had a terrifying hallucination; she tried to fend it off with her arm but was unable to do so. This gave her a violent fright, and for the time being the matter ended there. It was not until the outbreak of her hysteria that the contracture of the arm set in. In another woman patient, I observed that her speech was interrupted by a peculiar 'clacking' with her tongue, which resembled the cry of a capercaillie. I had been familiar with this symptom for months and regarded it as a *tic*. It was only after I once happened to question her under hypnosis about its origin that I discovered that the noise had first appeared on two occasions. On each of these she had made a firm decision to keep absolutely quiet. This happened once when she was nursing a child of hers who was seriously ill. (Nursing sick people often plays a part in the aetiology of hysteria.) The child had fallen asleep and she was determined not to make any noise that might wake it. But fear that she might make a noise turned into actually making one - an instance of 'hysterical counter-will'; she pressed her lips together and made the clacking noise with her tongue. Many years later the same symptom had arisen a second time, once again when she had made a decision to be absolutely quiet, and it had persisted ever afterwards. A single precipitating cause is often not enough to fixate a symptom; but if this same symptom appears several times accompanied by a particular affect, it becomes fixated and chronic.

One of the commonest symptoms of hysteria is a combination of anorexia and vomiting. I know of a whole number of cases in which the occurrence of this symptom is explained quite simply. Thus in one patient vomiting persisted after she had read a humiliating letter just before a meal and had been violently sick after it. In other cases disgust at food could be quite definitely related to the fact that, owing to the institution of the 'common table', a person may be compelled to eat his meal with someone he detests. The disgust is then transferred from the person to the food. The woman with the *tic* whom I have just mentioned was particularly interesting in this respect. She ate uncommonly little and only under pressure. I learnt from her in hypnosis that a series of psychical traumas had eventually produced this symptom of disgust at food. While she was still a child, her mother, who was very strict, insisted on her eating any meat she had left over at her midday meal two hours later, when it was cold and the fat was all congealed. She did so with great disgust and retained the memory of it; so that later on, when she was no longer subjected to this punishment, she regularly felt disgust at mealtimes. Ten years later she used to sit at table with a relative who was tubercular and kept constantly spitting across the table into the spitoon during meals. A little while later she was obliged to share her meals with a relative who, as she knew, was suffering from a contagious disease. Breuer's patient, again, behaved for some time like someone suffering from hydrophobia. During hypnosis it turned out that she had once unexpectedly seen a dog drinking out of a tumbler of water of hers.

Sleeplessness or disturbed sleep are also symptoms that are usually susceptible to the most precise explanation. Thus, for years on end a woman could never get to sleep till six in the morning. She had for a long time slept in the room adjoining her sick husband, who used to rise at six o'clock. After that hour she had been able to sleep in quiet; and she behaved in the same way once more many years later during a hysterical illness. Another case was that of a man. He was a hysterical patient who had slept very badly for the last twelve years. His sleeplessness, however, was of a quite special sort. In the summer he slept excellently, but in the winter very badly; and in November he slept quite particularly badly. He had no notion what this was due to. Enquiry revealed that in November twelve years earlier he had watched for many nights at the bedside of his son, who was ill with diphtheria.

Breuer's patient, to whom I have so often referred, offered an example of a disturbance of speech. For a long period of her illness she spoke only English and could neither speak nor understand German. This symptom was traced back to an event which had happened before the outbreak of her illness. While she was in a state of great anxiety, she had attempted to pray but could find no words. At last a few words of a child's prayer in English occurred to her. When she fell ill later on, only the English language was at her command.

The determination of the symptom by the psychical trauma is not so transparent in every instance. There is often only what may be described as a 'symbolic' relation between the determining cause and the hysterical symptom. This is especially true of pains. Thus one patient suffered from piercing pains between her eyebrows. The reason was that once when she was a child her grandmother had given her an enquiring, 'piercing' look. The same patient suffered for a time from violent pains in her right heel, for which there was no explanation. These pains, it turned out, were connected with an idea that occurred to the patient when she made her first appearance in society. She was overcome with fear that she might not 'find herself on a right footing'. Symbolizations of this kind were employed by many patients for a whole number of so-called neuralgias and pains. It is as though there were an intention to express the mental state by means of a physical one; and linguistic usage affords a bridge by which this can be effected. In the case, however, of what are after all the typical symptoms of hysteria- such as hemi-anaesthesia, restriction of the visual field, epileptiform convulsions, etc. - a psychical mechanism of this sort cannot be demonstrated. On the other hand this can often be done in respect to the hysterogenic zones.

These examples, which I have chosen out of a number of observations, seem to offer proof that the phenomena of common hysteria can safely be regarded as being on the same pattern as those of traumatic hysteria, with the involvement of psychical, as vs. actual physical trauma and that accordingly every hysteria can be looked upon as traumatic hysteria in the sense of implying a psychical trauma and that every hysterical phenomenon is determined by the nature of the trauma.

The further question which would then have to be answered is as to the nature of the causal connection between the determining factor which we have discovered during hypnosis and the phenomenon which persists subsequently as a chronic symptom. This connection might be of various kinds. It might be of the type that we should describe as a 'releasing' factor. For instance, if someone with a disposition to tuberculosis receives a blow on the knee as a result of which he develops a tubercular inflammation of the joint, the blow is a simple releasing cause. But this is not what happens in hysteria. There is another kind of causation - namely, *direct* causation. We can elucidate this from the picture of a foreign body, which continues to operate unceasingly as a stimulating cause of illness until it is got rid of. *Cessante causa cessat effectus.*[1] Breuer's observation shows us that there is a connection of this latter kind between the psychical trauma and the hysterical phenomenon. For Breuer learnt from his first patient that the attempt at discovering the determining cause of a symptom was at the same time a therapeutic manoeuvre. The moment at which the physician finds out the occasion when the symptom first appeared and the reason for its appearance is also the moment at which the symptom vanishes. When, for instance, the symptom presented by the patient consists in pains, and when we enquire from him under hypnosis as to their origin, he will produce a series of memories in connection with them. If we can succeed in eliciting a really vivid memory in him, and if he sees things before him with all their original actuality, we shall observe that he is completely dominated by some affect. And if we then compel him to put this affect into words, we shall find that, at the same time as he is producing this violent affect, the phenomenon of his pains emerges very markedly once again and that thenceforward the symptom, in its chronic character, disappears. This is how events turned out in all the instances I have quoted. And it was an interesting fact that the memory of this particular event was to an extraordinary degree more vivid than the memory of any others, and that the affect accompanying it was as great, perhaps, as it had been when the event actually occurred. It could only be supposed that the psychical trauma does in fact continue to operate in the subject and maintains the hysterical phenomenon, and that it comes to an end as soon as the patient has spoken about it.

As I have just said, if, in accordance with our procedure, one arrives at the psychical trauma by making enquiries from the patient under hypnosis, one discovers that the memory concerned is quite unusually strong and has retained the whole of its affect. The question now arises how it is that an event which occurred so long ago - perhaps ten or twenty years - can persist in exercising its power over the subject, how it is that these memories have not been subject to the processes of wearing away and forgetting.

[1] ['When the cause ceases the effect ceases']

With a view to answering this question, I should like to begin with a few remarks on the conditions which govern the wearing-away of the contents of our ideational life. We will start from a thesis that may be stated in the following terms. If a person experiences a psychical impression, something in his nervous system which we will for the moment call the sum of excitation is increased. Now in every individual there exists a tendency to diminish this sum of excitation once more, in order to preserve his health. The increase of the sum of excitation takes place along sensory paths, and its diminution along motor ones. So we may say that if anything impinges on someone he reacts in a motor fashion. We can now safely assert that it depends on this reaction how much of the initial psychical impression is left. Let us consider this in relation to a particular example. Let us suppose that a man is insulted, is given a blow or something of the kind. This psychical trauma is linked with an increase in the sum of excitation of his nervous system. There then instinctively arises an inclination to diminish this increased excitation immediately. He hits back, and then feels easier; he may perhaps have reacted adequately-that is, he may have got rid of as much as had been introduced into him. Now this reaction may take various forms. For quite slight increases in excitation, alterations in his own body may perhaps be enough: weeping, abusing, raging, and so on. The more intense the trauma, the greater is the adequate reaction. The most adequate reaction, however is always a deed. But, as an English writer has wittily remarked, the man who first flung a word of abuse at his enemy instead of a spear was the founder of civilization. Thus words are substitutes for deeds, and in some circumstances (e. g. in Confession) the only substitutes. Accordingly, alongside the adequate reaction there is one that is less adequate. If, however, there is no reaction *whatever* to a psychical trauma, the memory of it retains the affect which it originally had. So that if someone who has been insulted cannot avenge the insult either by a retaliatory blow or by a word of abuse, the possibility arises that the memory of the event may call up in him once more the affect which was originally present. An insult that has been repaid, even if only in words, is recollected quite differently from one that has had to be accepted; and linguistic usage characteristically describes an insult that has been suffered in silence as a 'mortification'. Thus, if for any reason there can be no reaction to a psychical trauma, it retains its original affect, and when someone cannot get rid of the increase in stimulation by 'abreacting' it, we have the possibility of the event in question remaining a psychical trauma. Incidentally, a healthy psychical mechanism has other methods of dealing with the affect of a psychical trauma even if motor reaction and reaction by words are denied to it - namely by working it over associatively and by producing contrasting ideas. Even if the person who has been insulted neither hits back nor replies with abuse, he can nevertheless reduce the affect attaching to the insult by calling up such contrasting ideas as those of his own worthiness, of his enemy's worthlessness, and so on. Whether a healthy man deals with an insult in one way or the other, he always succeeds in achieving the result that the affect which was originally strong in his memory eventually loses intensity and that finally the recollection, having lost its affect, falls a victim to forgetfulness and the process of wearing-away.

Now we have found that in hysterical patients there are nothing but impressions which have not lost their affect and whose memory has remained vivid. It follows, therefore, that these memories in hysterical patients, which have become pathogenic, occupy an exceptional position as regards the wearing-away process; and observation shows that, in the case of all the events which have become determinants of hysterical phenomena, we are dealing with psychical traumas which have not been completely abreacted, or completely dealt with. Thus we may assert that *hysterical patients suffer from incompletely abreacted psychical traumas.*

We find two groups of conditions under which memories become pathogenic. In the first group the memories to which the hysterical phenomena can be traced back have for their content ideas which involved a trauma so great that the nervous system had not sufficient power to deal with it in any way, or ideas to which reaction was impossible for social reasons (this applies frequently to married life); or lastly the subject may simply refuse to react, may not *want* to react to the psychical trauma. In this last case the contents of the hysterical deliria often turn out to be the very circle of ideas which the patient in his normal state has rejected, inhibited and suppressed with all his might.(For instance, blasphemies and erotic ideas occur in the hysterical deliria of nuns.) But in a second group of cases the reason for the absence of a reaction lies not in the content of the psychical trauma but in other circumstances. For we very often find that the content and determinants of hysterical phenomena are events which are in themselves quite trivial, but which have acquired high significance from the fact that they occurred at specially important moments when the patient's predisposition was pathologically increased. For instance, the affect of fright may have arisen in the course of some other severe affect and may on that account have attained such great importance. States of this kind are of short duration and are, as one might say, out of communication with the rest of the subject's mental life. While he is in a state of auto-hypnosis such as this, he cannot get rid associatively of an idea that occurs to him, as he can in a waking state. After considerable experience with these phenomena, we think it probable that in every hysteria we are dealing 'with a rudiment of what is called '*double conscience*', dual consciousness, and that a tendency to such a dissociation and with it the emergence of abnormal states of consciousness, which we propose to call 'hypnoid', is the basic phenomenon of hysteria.

Let us now consider the manner in which our therapy operates. It falls in with one of the dearest human wishes - the wish to be able to do something over again. Someone has experienced a psychical trauma without reacting to it sufficiently. We get him to experience it a second time, but under hypnosis; and we now compel him to complete his reaction to it. He can then get rid of the idea's affect, which was so to say 'strangulated', and when this is done the operation of the idea is brought to an end. Thus we cure - not hysteria but some of its individual symptoms - by causing an unaccomplished reaction to be completed.

You must not suppose, then, that very much has been gained by this for the therapeutics of hysteria. Hysteria, like the neuroses, has its deeper causes; and it is those deeper causes that set limits, which are often very appreciable, to the success of our treatment.